MW01416589

More
dump
&bake
Cakes

2-in-1 Cake Mix

Most recipes in this book use boxed cake mixes to prepare the dump cakes, but for a slightly different taste and texture, try this easy prep-ahead recipe. Simply use a portion of it in place of the regular cake mix listed in your recipe. Then store the remaining mixture in an airtight container for another cake.

In a large bowl, stir together 1 (16 oz.) pkg. angel food cake mix and 1 (15.25 oz.) pkg. golden vanilla cake mix (or another flavor) until well combined. Use about 2½ cups of this dry mixture in place of 1 (9 x 13") boxed cake mix. Makes enough for 2 cakes. (This mixture was used to prepare the dump cakes on pages 58 and 62.)

Copyright © 2015 CQ Products
Waverly, IA 50677
All rights reserved.
No part of this book may be reproduced or transmitted in any form or by any means, electronic or mechanical, including photocopying, recording or by any information storage and retrieval system, without permission in writing from the publisher.

Printed in the United States of America
by G&R Publishing Co.

Distributed By:

507 Industrial Street
Waverly, IA 50677

ISBN-13: 978-1-56383-523-0
Item #7122

Go beyond traditional dump cakes with these uniquely delicious layers of flavor. A dry cake mix plus a few simple ingredients are topped with buttery goodness right in a baking dish.

After baking, serve warm or cold and top with ice cream, whipped cream, powdered sugar, or frosting as desired. Whether scooped or cut, these easy cakes are company-worthy every time!

Helpful Hints

¤ Break up any lumps in the dry cake mix.

¤ Spread layers evenly for uniform baking.

¤ Pour liquid ingredients slowly and evenly over the cake mix to avoid dry spots.

¤ Butter may be added in three different ways: sliced, grated, or melted. Choose the method you like best, but be sure butter is well chilled if slicing or grating.

¤ Drizzle additional melted butter or other liquid over any dry areas during baking, or spritz with butter spray during the last 15 minutes of baking time.

¤ To reduce the calories, replace some of the butter with juice, water, or diet soda, or use fresh fruit instead of pie filling. (Note: Angel food cakes work best with regular soda.)

¤ Let cakes cool at least 30 minutes before serving. Most can be successfully refrigerated overnight.

Cranberry Delight

1 (20 oz.) can crushed pineapple, undrained

⅔ C. orange marmalade

1 (10 oz.) pkg. frozen cranberries, thawed

1 (16.5 oz.) pkg. pineapple cake mix

1 tsp. ground cardamom

2 tsp. cinnamon-sugar

½ C. butter, melted

Preheat oven to 350˚.
Lightly grease a 9 x 13" baking dish.

Layers

- ¤ Spread pineapple in prepared baking dish.
- ¤ Drop marmalade by the spoonful over pineapple.
- ¤ Scatter cranberries over fruit.
- ¤ Sprinkle dry cake mix, cardamom, and cinnamon-sugar evenly over cranberries.
- ¤ Drizzle melted butter over all.

Bake

50 to 55 minutes or until cake is golden brown.

Try

drizzling with cream cheese frosting.

Simply Apple

8 C. peeled, sliced apples

1 (18.25 oz.) pkg. yellow cake mix

½ C. butter, melted

½ C. apple cider

Preheat oven to 350˚.
Lightly grease a 9 x 13" baking dish.

Layers

- ¤ Arrange apple slices in prepared baking dish.
- ¤ Sprinkle dry cake mix evenly over apples.
- ¤ Drizzle with melted butter.
- ¤ Drizzle apple cider over all.

Bake

about 55 minutes or until top is brown and apples are tender.

Try

topping with cinnamon ice cream for a pie-like experience.

Strawberry-Rhubarb

1 (16 oz.) pkg. chopped frozen
   rhubarb (or 3 C. fresh)

2 (21 oz.) cans strawberry pie filling

2 T. lemon juice

1 (18.25 oz.) pkg. yellow cake mix

1 C. butter, melted

Preheat oven to 350˚.
Lightly grease a 9 x 13" baking dish.

Layers

- ⌗ Dump rhubarb and strawberry pie filling into prepared baking dish.

- ⌗ Add lemon juice and stir ingredients together until combined. Scrape down sides and spread evenly.

- ⌗ Sprinkle dry cake mix evenly over fruit.

- ⌗ Drizzle melted butter over all.

Bake

about 55 minutes or until deep golden brown and bubbly.

Mint Chip

1 (9 oz.) pkg. Jiffy white cake mix

⅓ C. half & half

2 egg whites

2 T. vegetable oil

½ C. chopped mint baking chips
(or creme de menthe chips)

⅓ C. Mallow Bits, plus more for
topping, optional

⅓ C. mint baking chips (not chopped)
for topping

Preheat oven to 350˚.
Lightly grease an 8 x 8" baking dish.

Layers

⌗   Dump dry cake mix in a mound in prepared baking dish and make a well in the center.

⌗   Add half & half, egg whites, and oil. Whisk ingredients together until well blended, scraping down sides.

⌗   Gently fold in chopped baking chips and ⅓ cup Mallow Bits, if desired. Spread batter evenly.

Bake

20 minutes and then top cake with whole baking chips and more Mallow Bits, if desired. Bake 2 to 4 minutes more, until chips are soft and cake tests done with a toothpick. Cool before cutting.

Try

drizzling with chocolate syrup just before serving.

peach Crumble

2 (15.25 oz.) cans sliced peaches in heavy syrup, undrained

1 (18.25 oz.) pkg. yellow cake mix

½ C. quick-cooking rolled oats

½ C. brown sugar

½ C. cold butter, thinly sliced

½ tsp. ground cinnamon

Preheat oven to 375°.
  Lightly grease a 9 x 13" baking dish.

Layers

- ✄ Dump peaches into prepared baking dish, spreading evenly.

- ✄ Sprinkle dry cake mix evenly over peaches and pat lightly.

- ✄ Sprinkle oats and brown sugar over cake mix.

- ✄ Arrange butter slices over the top and sprinkle with cinnamon.

Bake

40 to 45 minutes or until bubbly around edges.

Try

substituting two cans of apricots for the peaches.

Carrot Crunch

1 (20 oz.) can crushed pineapple, undrained

1 (15.25 oz.) pkg. carrot cake mix

½ C. raisins

1 C. apple juice

¾ C. sweetened flaked coconut

1 C. chopped walnuts

½ C. butter, melted

Preheat oven to 350˚.
  Lightly grease a 9 x 13" baking dish.

Layers

- ¤ Spread pineapple in prepared baking dish.

- ¤ Sprinkle dry cake mix evenly over fruit.

- ¤ Scatter raisins over cake mix.

- ¤ Drizzle apple juice over the top.

- ¤ Sprinkle with coconut and walnuts. Then drizzle melted butter over all.

Bake

35 to 40 minutes or until lightly browned and bubbly around edges.

 Try

topping with cream cheese frosting.

5-Layer

1 (17.9 oz.) pkg. Hershey's S'mores Cupcake Mix

¼ to ½ C. butter, melted

1 egg

1 (7 oz.) Hershey's Milk Chocolate candy bar, broken in pieces

¾ C. peanut butter chips

½ C. chopped walnuts

Preheat oven to 325 °.
Lightly grease a 9 x 9" baking dish.

Layers

- ¤ Dump both bags of dry ingredients from cupcake mix into prepared baking dish and make a well in the center.

- ¤ Add melted butter and egg to well. Stir until combined and then pat evenly in pan.

- ¤ Spread contents of marshmallow filling bag (from cupcake mix) over crust.

- ¤ Scatter candy bar pieces over marshmallow layer and sprinkle peanut butter chips and walnuts over all. Press down firmly.

Bake

25 to 30 minutes or until set and lightly browned.

Try

adding extra layers with butterscotch chips and/or toffee pieces.

Serves 15

ManDarin OranGe

1 (18.25 oz.) pkg. yellow cake mix

2 T. flour

1 (3 oz.) pkg. orange gelatin

4 eggs

½ C. vegetable oil

1 (15 oz.) can mandarin oranges, undrained

Preheat oven to 350˚.
 Lightly grease a 9 x 13" baking dish.

Layers

- ¤ Dump dry cake mix, flour, and dry gelatin into prepared baking dish. Stir together and make a well in the center.

- ¤ Add eggs, oil and mandarin oranges; stir until well blended, scraping down sides.

- ¤ Spread batter evenly.

Bake

30 to 35 minutes or until cake is lightly browned and tests done with a toothpick.

Try

topping with French Vanilla Cool Whip and adding a drizzle of warmed orange marmalade.

Serves 12–15

Sweet Potato

1 C. water

1 C. white grape juice

¾ C. sugar

1 tsp. vanilla extract

3 to 4 sweet potatoes, peeled and thinly sliced

¼ C. butter, melted

1 (15.25 oz.) pkg. yellow cake mix

½ C. cold butter, thinly sliced

Preheat oven to 300°.
Lightly grease a 9 x 13" baking dish.

Layers

- ⌘ Pour water, juice, sugar, and vanilla into prepared baking dish and stir to combine.

- ⌘ Arrange sweet potatoes in dish.

- ⌘ Drizzle with melted butter.

- ⌘ Sprinkle dry cake mix over the potatoes.

- ⌘ Arrange butter slices over the top.

Bake

60 to 70 minutes or until golden brown and bubbly. Let cool 8 hours or overnight.

Try

sprinkling each serving with mini marshmallows and browning briefly under a broiler.

Serves 12–15

Very Berry

2 (12 oz.) pkgs. frozen blackberries
   and/or raspberries, nearly thawed

1 (3 oz.) pkg. raspberry gelatin

⅓ C. sugar

1 (15.25 oz.) pkg. vanilla cake mix

½ C. chopped pecans

¾ C. butter, melted

½ C. water

Preheat oven to 350˚.
  Lightly grease a 9 x 13" baking dish.

Layers

- ¤ Spread blackberries evenly in prepared baking dish.

- ¤ Sprinkle gelatin and sugar over berries.

- ¤ Spread dry cake mix evenly over layers in dish and sprinkle with pecans.

- ¤ Drizzle melted butter over cake mix and pecans. Slowly pour water over all.

Bake

40 to 45 minutes or until golden brown and bubbly. Let cool before serving.

Try

using fresh berries, but then increase the water to 1 cup.

Peach-Berry

6 C. peeled, sliced fresh peaches (6 large)

4 C. sliced fresh strawberries

1 C. sugar

¼ C. flour

1 tsp. ground cinnamon

1 (15.25 oz.) pkg. golden butter cake mix

⅔ C. butter, melted

Preheat oven to 350˚.
  Lightly grease a 9 x 13" baking dish.

Layers

- ⌗ Dump peaches and strawberries into prepared baking dish.

- ⌗ Sprinkle sugar and flour over fruit. Stir until well combined, scraping down sides; spread evenly.

- ⌗ Sprinkle with cinnamon and dry cake mix.

- ⌗ Drizzle melted butter over all.

Bake

  about 55 minutes or until golden brown and bubbly.

Try

serving with whipped cream and sliced fresh strawberries

Lime Jello No-Poke

1 (18.25 oz.) pkg. white cake mix

3 egg whites

⅓ C. vegetable oil

1¼ C. lemon sparkling water

½ (3 oz.) pkg. lime gelatin (about 3 T.)

6 vanilla or lemon sandwich cookies, crushed

Preheat oven to 350˚.
Lightly grease a 9 x 13" baking dish.

Layers

- ⌑ Dump dry cake mix in a mound in prepared baking dish. Make a well in the center and add egg whites, oil, and sparkling water. Whisk ingredients together until well blended. Scrape down sides and spread evenly.

- ⌑ Sprinkle dry gelatin over cake batter. Gently swirl gelatin through batter with a fork.

- ⌑ Scatter cookie crumbs over the top.

Bake

30 to 35 minutes or until cake tests done with a toothpick. Cool before cutting.

Try

topping with whipped cream and a sprinkle of lime zest.

Piña ColaDa AnGel FooD

1 (16 oz.) pkg. angel food cake mix

1 (20 oz.) can crushed pineapple, undrained

1 (8 oz.) tub whipped topping, thawed

½ C. toasted coconut (raw chips or sweetened flakes)

Preheat oven to 350˚.
  Use an ungreased 9 x 13" baking dish.

Layers

¤ Dump dry cake mix into prepared baking dish and make a well in the center.

¤ Add pineapple to well and stir together until thoroughly blended.

¤ Scrape down sides and spread batter evenly in dish.

Bake

25 to 30 minutes, until golden brown and set. Cool completely. Spread with whipped topping and sprinkle with coconut before serving.

Serves 12–15

Raspberry Fizz

2 (12 oz.) pkgs. frozen raspberries

1 (15.25 oz.) pkg. white cake mix

2 C. lemon-lime soda

1 (2 oz.) pkg. macadamia nuts, chopped (about ½ C.)

½ C. milk chocolate chips

½ C. white baking chips

Preheat oven to 350˚.
  Lightly grease a 9 x 13" baking dish.

Layers

- ✠ Dump frozen raspberries into prepared baking dish, spreading evenly.

- ✠ Sprinkle dry cake mix evenly over raspberries.

- ✠ Drizzle lemon-lime soda over all.

- ✠ Sprinkle macadamia nuts, chocolate chips, and white baking chips on top and cover dish with foil.

Bake

20 minutes. Uncover and bake 25 to 35 minutes longer or until golden brown and bubbly around edges. Cool before serving.

 Try

topping with fresh raspberries.

PistaChio CreaM

1 (18.25 oz.) pkg. white cake mix

1 (3.4 oz.) pkg. pistachio instant pudding mix

1 (20 oz.) can crushed pineapple,
  juice reserved

About ½ C. additional pineapple juice

3 eggs

½ C. plus 2 T. chopped roasted & salted
  pistachios, divided

½ C. cold butter, thinly sliced

Preheat oven to 350°.
Lightly grease a 9 x 13" baking dish.

Layers

- ⧓ Dump dry cake mix and pudding mix in a mound in prepared baking dish and make a well in the center.

- ⧓ Combine reserved juice from pineapple with enough extra pineapple juice to measure 1½ cups liquid. Add the liquid and eggs to well; whisk together until well blended.

- ⧓ Stir in pineapple and ¼ cup pistachios. Scrape down sides and spread batter evenly in dish.

- ⧓ Arrange butter slices over the top and sprinkle with remaining pistachios.

Bake

35 to 40 minutes or until cake tests done with a toothpick. Cool completely.

Try

spreading cream cheese frosting over the top and sprinkling with more pistachios.

Apricot Cobbler

1 (24 oz.) can apricot halves in light syrup, undrained

1 (15.25 oz.) pkg. butter pecan cake mix

½ C. cold butter

¾ C. brown sugar

¾ to 1 C. granola cereal

Preheat oven to 350˚.
Lightly grease a 9 x 13" baking dish.

Layers

- ⌗ Pour apricots into prepared baking dish and cut the fruit into small pieces.
- ⌗ Sprinkle dry cake mix evenly over apricots.
- ⌗ Grate butter evenly over the top.
- ⌗ Sprinkle with brown sugar and granola.

Bake

about 40 minutes. Serve warm or cold.

 Try

topping with cinnamon ice cream.

Cherry Chip

1 (15.25 oz.) pkg. cherry chip cake mix

¼ C. vegetable oil

3 eggs

1 C. Mountain Dew or lemon-lime soda

1 (12 oz.) pkg. frozen tart red cherries,
    thawed and drained

1½ C. coarsely chopped pecan sandy cookies

3 T. butter, melted

Preheat oven to 350°.
   Lightly grease a 9 x 13" baking dish.

Layers

☼ Dump dry cake mix in a mound in prepared baking dish and make a well in the center.

☼ Add oil, eggs, and Mountain Dew to well and whisk together until thoroughly blended. Spread batter evenly in dish, scraping down sides.

☼ Scatter cherries over cake batter.

☼ Sprinkle cookie crumbs over the top and drizzle with melted butter.

Bake

about 35 minutes or until cake tests done with a toothpick. Cool completely.

 Try

drizzling frosting over cake and serving with cherry ice cream.

Lemon Poppy Seed

1 (22 oz.) can lemon pie filling

1 (15.25 oz.) pkg. lemon cake mix, divided

½ C. cold butter, thinly sliced, divided

1 to 2 tsp. poppy seed

⅓ C. sliced almonds

Use a buttered 3-quart slow cooker.

Layers

- ⌑ Spread lemon pie filling in the bottom of prepared slow cooker.

- ⌑ Spread half the dry cake mix over pie filling. Arrange half the butter slices over cake mix.

- ⌑ Top with remaining cake mix and remaining butter slices.

- ⌑ Sprinkle evenly with poppy seed and almonds. Cover with lid.

Bake

about 4 hours on LOW or until center of cake tests done with a toothpick.

Try

serving in dessert cups with a dollop of whipped cream on top.

Serves 15–20

Cherry Cola

1 (21 oz.) can cherry pie filling

1 (15.25 oz.) pkg. dark chocolate
  cake mix

1 C. cherry cola

¾ to 1 C. chocolate chunks

Preheat oven to 350˚.
Lightly grease a 9 x 13" baking dish.

Layers

✠ Spread cherry pie filling in prepared baking dish.

✠ Sprinkle dry cake mix over pie filling.

✠ Drizzle cola over the top, and without disturbing fruit, stir gently until mostly blended.

✠ Carefully sprinkle chocolate chunks over the top.

Bake

35 to 40 minutes or until bubbly around edges.

Serves 12–15

OranGe Tutti-Frutti

1 (20 oz.) can crushed pineapple, undrained

1 (15 oz.) can fruit cocktail, undrained

¼ C. drained, chopped maraschino cherries

1 (15.25 oz.) pkg. orange cake mix

2 (1.23 oz.) packets instant apple-cinnamon oatmeal (from a 12.3 oz. box)

1 C. natural raw chip coconut

¾ C. butter, melted

Preheat oven to 350°.
  Lightly grease a 9 x 13" baking dish.

Layers

- ✠ Spread pineapple, fruit cocktail, and cherries evenly in prepared baking dish.

- ✠ Sprinkle dry cake mix evenly over fruit.

- ✠ Scatter oatmeal over cake mix and sprinkle with coconut.

- ✠ Drizzle melted butter over all.

Bake

about 50 minutes or until golden brown.

Try

serving with a dollop of French Vanilla Cool Whip and a maraschino cherry on top.

ReD Velvet

1 (15.25 oz.) pkg. red velvet cake mix

1 (3.4 oz.) pkg. vanilla instant
   pudding mix

1½ C. milk

1 C. white chocolate baking chips

15 raspberry Hugs candies,
   unwrapped

¼ C. chopped macadamia nuts

Preheat oven to 350°.
Lightly grease a 9 x 13" baking dish.

Layers

- ☐ Dump dry cake mix and pudding mix into prepared baking dish.

- ☐ Make a well in the center of dry ingredients and add milk. Whisk together until well blended and thick, but still lumpy. Scrape down sides and spread batter evenly.

- ☐ Scatter baking chips over batter.

- ☐ Chop the candies and sprinkle evenly over the top.

- ☐ Sprinkle nuts over all.

Bake

about 35 minutes or until cake pulls away from sides of pan and tests done with a toothpick. Let cool.

Try

drizzling with melted white baking chips.

chocolate-marshmallow

1 (15.75 oz.) can ready-to-eat chocolate pudding

5 or 6 whole graham crackers

½ C. mini semi-sweet chocolate chips

1 (15.25 oz.) pkg. milk chocolate cake mix

½ C. cold butter, thinly sliced

⅓ C. fat-free half & half

Butter spray, optional

40 large marshmallows

Preheat oven to 350˚.
  Lightly grease a 9 x 13" baking dish.

Layers

□ Spread chocolate pudding in
    prepared baking dish.

□ Break graham crackers in half or
    quarters and arrange over pudding,
    leaving space between them.

□ Sprinkle with chocolate chips.

□ Sprinkle dry cake mix evenly over
    layers in dish.

□ Arrange butter slices over the top.
    Then drizzle half & half over all.

Bake

about 25 minutes, spraying any dry
areas with butter spray partway
through baking time, if desired.
Arrange marshmallows on top
and bake 10 to 12 minutes more,
until golden brown. Serve warm.

Autumn Spice

2 (21 oz.) cans apple pie filling

1 tsp. ground cinnamon

1 tsp. ground nutmeg

½ tsp. ground allspice

1 T. sugar

1 (15.25 oz.) pkg. spice cake mix

¾ C. cold butter, thinly sliced

1 C. chopped pecans

Preheat oven to 350°.
  Lightly grease a 9 x 13" baking dish.

Layers

- ⌑ Spread apple pie filling in prepared baking dish.
- ⌑ Sprinkle cinnamon, nutmeg, allspice and sugar evenly over pie filling.
- ⌑ Spread dry cake mix over spices.
- ⌑ Arrange butter slices over the top.
- ⌑ Scatter pecans over all.

Bake

40 to 45 minutes or until golden brown on top and bubbly around edges.

Try

scooping into bowls and serving warm with vanilla ice cream.

Gingerbread

1 (23 oz.) jar applesauce

1 (20 oz.) can crushed pineapple, undrained

¼ C. cinnamon-sugar

1 (14.5 oz.) pkg. Gingerbread Cake & Cookie Mix

1 C. butter, melted

½ C. chopped pecans

1 C. coarsely chopped gingersnap cookies

Preheat oven to 350˚.
  Lightly grease a 9 x 13" baking dish.

Layers

- ¤ Spread applesauce in prepared baking dish.

- ¤ Spread pineapple evenly over applesauce and sprinkle with cinnamon-sugar.

- ¤ Spread dry cake mix evenly over fruit.

- ¤ Drizzle with melted butter.

- ¤ Sprinkle with pecans and cookie crumbs.

Bake

40 to 45 minutes or until browned and bubbly.

Serves 9

Strawberry-Pineapple

1 (8 oz.) can crushed pineapple, undrained

3 C. sliced fresh strawberries

2 to 2½ T. dry strawberry gelatin

1 (9 oz.) pkg. Jiffy yellow cake mix

½ C. chopped pecans

⅓ C. butter, melted

Preheat oven to 350°.
Lightly grease a 9 x 9" baking dish.

Layers

- ✢ Spread pineapple in prepared baking dish. Arrange strawberries over pineapple.

- ✢ Sprinkle fruit with dry gelatin.
- ✢ Sprinkle dry cake mix evenly over fruit.
- ✢ Scatter pecans over the top.
- ✢ Drizzle melted butter over all.

Bake

25 to 30 minutes or until bubbly around edges.

Try

rhubarb or raspberries and raspberry gelatin in place of strawberries and strawberry gelatin.

scotcheroo

1 (15.25 oz.) pkg. white cake mix

1 (3.4 oz.) pkg. butterscotch instant pudding mix

3 eggs

½ C. sour cream

¾ C. lemon-lime soda

½ C. creamy peanut butter, warmed for drizzling

¼ C. butter, melted

1 C. milk chocolate chips

½ C. butterscotch chips

Preheat oven to 350˚.
  Lightly grease a 9 x 13" baking dish.

Layers

✠ Dump dry cake mix and pudding mix into prepared baking dish and stir together. Make a well in the center of dry ingredients.

✠ Add eggs, sour cream, and lemon-lime soda to well; whisk together until thoroughly blended, scraping down sides. Spread batter evenly in dish.

✠ Drizzle peanut butter and butter over cake batter.

✠ Sprinkle chocolate and butterscotch chips over all.

Bake

25 to 30 minutes or until cake is golden brown around edges and tests done with a toothpick. Cool before cutting.

Serves 15

SalteD Caramel Chocolate

1 C. milk

1 (3.4 oz.) pkg. vanilla instant pudding mix

½ C. caramel ice cream topping

1 (18.25 oz.) pkg. devil's food cake mix

2 eggs

¼ C. butter, melted

3 (2.5 oz.) bags mini Rolos candies

Coarse sea salt for sprinkling

Preheat oven to 350°.
Lightly grease a 9 x 13" baking dish.

Layers

- ¤ Pour milk into prepared baking dish. Add dry pudding mix and caramel topping. Whisk together until smooth and well blended.

- ¤ Dump dry cake mix in a mound on pudding layer. Make a well in the center and add eggs. Whisk all ingredients together until well blended, scraping down sides. Spread batter evenly in dish.

- ¤ Drizzle with melted butter.

- ¤ Arrange Rolos over the top and sprinkle very lightly with sea salt.

Bake

30 to 35 minutes or until cake tests done with a toothpick. Cool before serving.

Try

drizzling with caramel and topping with whipped cream and more Rolos.

Cherry-Pineapple Deluxe

1 (21 oz.) can cherry pie filling

1 (20 oz.) can crushed pineapple, undrained

2½ C. dry 2-in-1 Cake Mix*

¾ C. dark chocolate chips

1 to 1½ C. sweetened flaked coconut

¾ C. chopped walnuts

1 C. butter, melted

* Find the recipe for 2-in-1 Cake Mix at the
  front of this book.

Preheat oven to 350˚.
Lightly grease a 9 x 13" baking dish.

Layers

- ♯ Spread cherry pie filling in prepared baking dish.

- ♯ Cover pie filling with pineapple.

- ♯ Sprinkle dry cake mix evenly over fruit.

- ♯ Scatter chocolate chips, coconut, and walnuts evenly over the top.

- ♯ Drizzle with melted butter.

Bake

about 40 minutes or until golden brown and bubbly.

Try

substituting a vanilla or yellow cake mix for the 2-in-1 Cake Mix.

Raspberry-Hot FuDGe

2 (21 oz.) cans raspberry pie filling

1 (15.25 oz.) pkg. vanilla cake mix

¾ C. butter, melted

1 (12.8 oz.) jar hot fudge ice cream
   topping, warmed according to
   directions on jar

Preheat oven to 350°.
  Lightly grease a 9 x 13" baking dish.

Layers

- ¤ Spread raspberry pie filling in prepared baking dish.
- ¤ Sprinkle dry cake mix evenly over pie filling.
- ¤ Drizzle melted butter and hot fudge topping over all.

Bake

1 hour or until bubbly around edges.

Try

topping with fresh berries and serving warm or cold with ice cream.

Banana-Pear

2 (15 oz.) cans sliced pears, undrained

2 ripe bananas, sliced

2½ C. dry 2-in-1 Cake Mix*

½ C. cold butter, thinly sliced

Cinnamon-sugar

* Find the recipe for 2-in-1 Cake Mix at
  the front of this book.

Preheat oven to 350˚.
Lightly grease a 9 x 13" baking dish.

Layers

✠ Pour pears into prepared baking dish and cut them into smaller pieces as needed.

✠ Arrange banana slices evenly over the pears, pressing them lightly into the juice.

✠ Spread dry cake mix evenly over fruit.

✠ Arrange butter slices over the top. Sprinkle evenly with cinnamon-sugar.

Bake

about 40 minutes. Serve within a day or two.

Try

brushing banana slices with citrus juice or Fruit Fresh mixed with water to prevent browning.

InDex